The Beauty behind Her Ladyship

The One Altogether Cherish

By

Bernard Benson Sarfo

Also by Bernard Benson Sarfo

The Fact Among Facts (1st)
The Fact Among Facts

Standalone
The Youth Murderer
Be Original Not a Copy
The Christians Science or Scholarship
Precious than Paradise
Habit Makes Future
A shelter from storm and rain
The Science of Life
The Strongest Lion Knockback
The Perfect and Inspiring City
Above Hope, Faith and Love
The Hero's Brave Decisions
The Weakest Among Plants
The Hero's Brave Decisions
Doing Above The Ability
The Wisdom Beyond Power And Greatness
Heavier Than the Heavens
The Academics Brains and Recreation Logics
The Strange Voice

The Chaotic World
Don't Miss Your Flight
Let the Nations Ponder
You Are Your Thoughts
I AM has sent me to you
Life Tools
The Fact Among Facts
You Are Glorified
The Life Cinema
The Victims of Lifelong Slavery
The Beauty behind Her Ladyship

Dedication

I dedicate this book to the women in the world today and wish them well!

'When wisdom entered into your heart, and knowledge is pleasant unto your soul, discretion shall preserve you, understanding shall keep you' (Proverbs 2:10, 11).

Introduction

In the beginning God created the heavens and the earth. Human beings are the crown being in all the creatures that God made. Woman was the latest in the creation. Her creation made world complete and certain.

Woman is the second self of a man, beautiful and most attractive nature among the creatures of the world. Woman is the mother of all human beings existed today.

It is woman that give birth to men and women. In fact, it is through women that makes the world. The man was alone at the beginning of his life. It is abysmal and sad to be single.

The joy and the life of a man were meaningless at the beginning through the absences of a woman. God saw that, it is not good for a man to be single.

So, God made a woman fit and help for man. The happiness of a man made whole because of a woman. Woman was a second self and a help for a man. The whole world satisfied for the creation of a woman. Man was not a man without woman at that time. That is, his life became lifeless through the absences of a woman. Women are the world, and the worlds are women.

The trees; birds, rivers and cattle wasn't the man's happiness but the woman who fulfill his joy for the first time he saw her. Women can control the world for good and can control the world for bad.

What is women satisfaction? What makes them satisfy? What is their interest? What are they looking for? What pleased them? These questions will let us know what the women want in the world we live.

Today, Women love beauty than uniqueness and love joy and happiness than peace. They prefer sweets and comfort to sensitivity. They love show and glory than humility.

It is their wish to be on top than truthfulness. They love comfort but prevent to do well. They love pampered than principles. Nothing satisfies them but always want more.

I want women to be women than nothing and wished them good and best than expression.

It is difficult to explain the relation of bond between man and woman as one flesh in the marriage institution.

But it is reasonable to know the main idea that the marriage was established by God. Many people do not know the purpose and the uniqueness of marriage.

The solemnization of marriage is beyond calculation of anything that can be calculated. Marriage is beyond the world that can be called world or globe. If there is a world, then it is a marriage. If there is no marriage, then there is no world.

In the beginning God created the Heavens and the Earth. The purpose of this world created by God was fulfilled by marriage. Yet, the marriage is the most honorable thing in the world than anything established by God.

The world cannot be the world without marriage. It is a basic or source of human development which makes the world reasonable and necessary. So, the world became reasonable through human existence. It is a greatest sin to disregard marriage.

The world was created for a man but it became necessary through marriage. The reason is that, it is not good for a man to live alone; yet, it is good for a man to have a partner or the helper fit for his life.

The beauty is that, the man and the woman will be one flesh but not as different beings. This makes the reason of a marriage as it name meaningful and fruitful.

It is also makes us understand the unity of God heads as one. Marriage let us understand the uniqueness of God as one but with three persons. This makes the relationship of a man and woman reasonable and understandable. Though, the man bend woman are two different persons in shape but one flesh in all moves.

This book will let us know the peak idea of marriage and how it must be honored. It is an institution that makes human production and the world reasonable to live in.

It is a serious business which nothing can be compare in the lives of men. How have you considered marriage? How do you take it for?

It is a life and the death matter which no one must joke with. It depends on reason to marry but not as grant in any way which benefits the needs and wants of life. It needs understanding; knowledge and reason to go into marriage. So, everyone must understand the way of marriage before getting into it. You should not go in as thought but preparation and well mature mind to be in marriage.

Those engage in marriage must have a reasonable and thought. It is a big thing than what you can imagine and considered. Let us consider the following and know the best way to enter in marriage.

Contents

18. Oh my dear!

1. Why women?

Women are wonderfully made and resemble man in blood; body and spirit. Their structure is different from man but the same flesh and blood. Woman is a second self of a man in image and likeness with the same blood and flesh.

Why women as the content of this page and I am writing? There are a lot to say about women. Women are men's help, fit and beauty as well. They are unique in creation and complex to handle.

They are God's latest creature in all creation. Their attitude is a quiet different from men but the same being. They are nice but weak in doing and in behavior. God instructed man at the beginning of their creation.

Man is the head and manager of creatures. His duty is to care and keep; subdue and have dominion over all creatures. It came to pass, one day the devil approach the woman and entice her to disobey the instruction given to them.

Through the disobedient of the instruction given to them, woman became the subject of the devil. She tempted her husband and both became sinners. The world wasn't like this as we feel today. It was peaceful; comfortable, order and happiness.

Women have become the world in all things which are named. They are the seed; the tree and the fruit. Means they are part of everything that goes on in our world today.

Whether good or bad; positive or negative, partial or impartial and the others; in fact, they are part of everything that needs to be done or not. You cannot avoid them and without them things will not be totally done.

Women love beauty than principles and comfort than peace. They love joy and happiness than truthfulness. They also take things for granted; whether the outcome will be good or not.

Means they sometimes do not think to act. Rather they act before thinking. They are curious and wish to test everything. They are weak but nice; helpful but with fault, less in prudent but high in pretense.

Sin has degraded them in art; knowledge and glory. They sometimes act like babies and love pampered than correction. They always want to challenge themselves and wish grudge than peace.

It is interesting that they do not care sometimes when they stumble or err. I always shock when I see women struggling on things without considering. Women are complex but helpful no doubt about it. They are unique but out of order.

They love beauty but prevent good name and manners, prefer to make a mistake than to correct. They always want more and does not know sufficient. They are fast to love envy than to love any condition or contentment.

They do not know satisfaction and do not accept what they have, but always seek above the wish. Oh women! What do you need? What sufficient you?

Envy cannot lead you to anywhere; neither world goods can solve your problems. But the woman who fears God will be worthy praise.

It is my wish to let you know some of your condition and doings something about it. To let you know the best for your soul. May God give you understanding as we continue reading of this book messages.

2. Protect your ladyship

Women want beauty and joy; and want the best out of the greatest. But good name is better than the possessions and peace is better than the worrying.

It is peak and honor to fall on the pit than to sleep in the waves of the sea. That is, be sufficient or accept your rag than somebody's cloth which is abominable to be wash.

Means keep yourself from unquenchable fire and sleep on your old house. Consider yourself in this life and know where to step your foot. Do not rush in life but walk; you will reach your destination.

What is the matter? What do you need? Many have die because of their wish. Others have lost their dignity because of flesh.

Do not throw yourself into ground whiles you haven't hated any stone by your leg. But open your eyes and look forward and prevent accident. What does your lust will lead you to? What will benefit you, if you lost your ladyship? Be a lady among ladies and woman among thousands of women. Means keep yourself from all dishonesty and be an object lesson to others. Do not let others paint your face for you, but paint your own face as suit your beauty.

Means do not let others take you for granted by means of your weakness. But approve yourself as a work lady who is able to do for her own. Do not be enticed by men with their small amount of money that cannot buy you a life.

But fear God and know how to behavior in front of Him. Means, be a lady in all matters of life and accept your condition; yet your set time will fulfill.

Do not rush men, nor give yourself to them. But allow God to set your head for you in the time of your need. Then you will be a head woman among the women but not a tail woman among the women.

Do not harm yourself for money sake but harm yourself for Christ Jesus sake. Protect your ladyship. Never follow mouth but follow wisdom and knowledge about your future.

Why are you kissing the dust, instead of water? Why are you eating sand, instead of food? Do not cross the road without looking side and side. This means, be vigilant and wait for due time, but do not rush into marriage you do not know the end.

Be smart but not as a fool; think but do not over think, dress but not as a fornicator. Though, many of the women are doing that, but what should I do as a lady? Ask yourself? What will they say, if I separate myself from them?

Oh! You are too much, you are too much. But then should I go as they go? Should I walk as they walk? Should I dress as they dress? What identifies me?

What am I doing? What differences am I making? What will be the end result? What do I want you to learn? Why all these questions? You need to consider and act and look before throwing.

Else, you will hate someone unaware. Women must notice every act and manage every condition that they are in. Ladies who are purely ladies does not wear rag with fit cloth but wear fit clothes that suit occasion. Means protect your name for God sake but not your wish!

3. Stop deception

Women love pretense than to work from heart. Some wish to lie and survive than telling the truth and die in it. Do not move as you have not intended but move with intention.

That is, do not pretend as you love because of money, but love whiles there is no money, and build your life well. Do not love by your mouth but love from your heart.

Do not hesitate to tell the truth but tell the truth without intention. Means do not fear to tell the truth and do not consider death whiles you are telling the truth.

Else, you will stop telling the truth. Women appear sometimes as lovers but refuse to promote it. Do not dress as light or angel with the shadow behind your back.

Be forceful and do well, whiles there is no one at your place. But do not work as a forceful woman before your husband or anyone, whiles you know it is not from your heart that you are doing.

Do well and be impartial in greeting with your colleagues. Stop deception. Do not wear two clothes at the same time but one at a time.

Means do not close your eyes and do things as a mad woman and later say you are sorry. Do not fight as without reason, but fight with a reasonable case and be accepted with all who heard it.

Do not sing a bird song, whiles you know it is against your sister or someone else. Never walk or dance to display your happiness before trees in your house, whiles you know it is against your neighbor.

Do not shout without calling someone, whiles you know it goes contrary to your house mate. Women, it is not as you think but it is as you wish it to be in your own sight.

Do not throw dust in the air whiles you know it is raining. Means do not say words that are not true in the time of peace. But consider that moment and let the rain continue in peace. Stop pretending;

Live wisely and prevent chaos. Women, it is dangerous to pretend than even lie with your mouth. Deceptions are now rampant in all that we are doing.

People deceive to make money; others deceive to kill innocents. Deception is more than killings and it destroys entire world.

It does not suit you to deceive oh women! It is not fit to be pretender. But it fit you to tell the truth and love peace. Deception is above all wickedness and it is dangerous to be a deceiver.

It is the tool of the devil and the seat of his kingdom difficult to find out. Everyone who deceives or pretends is in the position of the devil. So, women do not allow this act to overtake you as a thief.

If you are practicing this kind of act, then you have join hand with the devil. Charming becomes the brother of deception when it avoid the truth.

So, it is serious to pretend as light, whiles you know it is not so. Women, do not allow the devil to use you but do your best to prevent this act by the grace of God.

Your beauty is your character and your falsehoods are your ruin. Consider your actions and do not deceive. Stop pretense and love truth.

4. Be a prudent woman

Now many women are doing things that are questionable. It is not their fault but it is how they want it to be. Why you are doing that? What do you want in this life?

Why are you disgracing yourself? What is your problem? Do you know you are the image of God and His likeness? Do things right and open your eyes; you are woman the latest creature of God.

You are current in the creation. You are genuine and wonderful. You are shock to men and dear before them. Maintain your dignity and beauty such supersedes all creation on the earth.

Do not be an artificial woman, but be natural and original that suits your beauty. Do not disgrace yourself because of money.

Be a virtuous woman and know how to control yourself. Do sensible things and make others pride because of you. Let people ask others of your good behavior.

Who is this woman? Where did she stay? Whose daughter? Where her family comes from? Let people who are worthy seek and ask for you. Be forceful in your work and do what you can. Do not measure your work with time but work according to your ability.

Do not waste time and do not be a lazy. Be practical and do your best that suits your energy. Stop gossiping and do not find faults with others.

Think for yourself but mind others through giving. Considering your act each moment and be aware of yourself for good.

Do not close your eyes and wear any cloth but open your eyes and be decent. Do not lie for favor but do your best to avoid poverty.

Try to prevent mismanagements and value the little you have. Do not waste your time on useless communications but value time and make use of each moment.

Be alert to help and do good to others who are weak. Never be partial but know how to deal with others who are short in appearance.

Do the right thing but not above the principles. Consider and mind your doings. Do not be haste to answer a question but be a little slower of your reply to prevent injury.

Be prepared to avoid distrust and always learn and build your ability. Do not pretend as you know everything but be a learner and keep your value.

Be a natural woman and then prevent accident. Do your things well and prepare your room with right lotions to prevent stink that prevent others from you.

Means, be decent in all your doings and have good report at your back. Do not appear as a harlot but be woman with good air. Remember that nothing is free that do not have price at least but be watchful and build your house well.

Do not chase men as a female dog in your time of ovulation but keep yourself to prevent shamefulness. Do not be too pompons but be modest in all your appearance.

Do not laugh at poor woman but do your best to help her, if you can. For you do not know what is coming. Who knows, maybe one day a servant will ride horse.

Do not make ways for yourself to allow dogs into your room. But close it and make windows for yourself to allow good air into your room.

Means do not make friends for nothing but make good friends for your future joy and glory. Why are you dismantling your diamond that have price?

Why are you selling your gold that supersedes wealth? Do not make yourself dirty and blame God at the end; for it is your own choice. Know how to talk to each one and build your foundation well.

Means consider your speech first when you are communicating to others and let them admire your presence. Respect but not as a fool; that is know the time and hour that demand decorum of approach with correct air to prevent shamefulness.

It is good to greet someone or others but it is not good to greet all the time. Else, people will notice you as an indecent woman. Women! You are wonderful made and excel in all creation.

Build yourself in the manner that has no questions and answers and be a woman of value. Be a prudent woman and prove your beautiful character. Mean it and make it well.

5. Weak vessel but attractive

Women are weak but attractive for good and evil. They are weak but not weak as nothing; but of good value. They are vessel that carries goods and sweets.

Without them men will be speechless. They are weak in all matters of life but they are value more than precious pearl. Women do not mind to hurt.

They always want to challenge themselves and hate words or disagree with words that are not in their favor. They want sweets than better and cherish comfort than harmony.

They lack forgiving spirit and want others fall than their progress. They are charmers but fault alarms with soundless beat. They love show but hate price.

It is hard to know what they want or need. They show less in appreciation but demand than supply. They are weak but can move the entire world.

Their absence cools things down on the occasion and fire gone when they are not at home. They are very complex but fit and helpful. They do not mind to act negatively with no sorry.

Their attractiveness calls for peace but not in them. They cool down fire but they are fire. It is difficult to identify them but good in supporting.

Women are gorgeous but weak; helpful but questions, manageable but regardless in doing. Women love words than questions and complain than correcting.

They love conversation than implementation. Women are weak vessel but attractive in manners sometimes. They love belongings but refuse to pay for.

It is their wish to be on top but fail to work towards it. Some of them do not want to learn anything but want the best. They are easy to convince and cheap to trap.

They are weak but attractive in supporting. Women! You are not with your own but you have been bought with price by Jesus Christ. You can do something about this condition and make things good and welcome. You are the world and the world is you today.

What difference can you make as an individual? Your act and move can change the world for good; and it can change the world for evil.

What manner of character are you building? Who are you? What is your name? (Oh women!)

You need to stand firm and build the broken bones and the flesh. It is you not the other one; you can start something towards change of situation that is abysmal.

Someone wants to see your move and then follows you. You can do something and let the world admire you. Stand up and move for change in attitude; for change in character, for change in dress, for change in speech, for change in learning and good name.

You can charm the world with your good behavior and build the broken old house. Means it stands on you for peace in the world; it stands on you for Christ to come prompt. Be not just a woman but a woman of Christ!

6. Nice but faulty

Women are lovely made and very helpful to men in terms of marriage. They are keys in life and all life matters. They are curious and always want something that is enjoyable.

They love to be happy all the time and always wish good life. It is their wish to be pampered all the time by men. But what makes them carelessness.

They easy to deceive or trick in the sense that, they do not think ahead what shall it be or what will be happen incase doing this thing or that? Due to their quick acts, makes them impatient and easy to err in their doings all the time. They want things fast them to think of the outcome.

Their wish demand and quick to act with no questions and answers. That is make it done and let them have their part. They love joy but consider little of the results.

Nice but faulty; helpful but impatient, curious but bad results. If women will have patient in doing; in talking, in dressing and others matters, they will bring sky down.

Means they can do wonderful things that supersede the men. Let women consider this; impatient have made them faulty and less in doing the good thing.

It is beautiful to note that, women have more chance and favor them the men in all ages. Women, do not let men look down on you or let them shout on you because of impatient or careless act.

Women can make the world like honey on the bases of your beautiful character and with good attitude. You are the first teacher of your children's and the mother of all the men.

Let women look at their beauty and then glorify God in all their doings. They need to be considerate and honest in all their doings. It is a disgrace for women to dress anyhow without the fear of God and appear as if eyeless or blind.

You are the builder of human families and the world song that wools the heart of the men. You should not throw away your beauty and the glory of your being.

You (women) do not let men say; women, women as we sometime heard off. But let men say; oh my dear! You are among the thousands and you are my joy and happiness. Let women put aside furious talk and build their house with integrity; love and patience.

Women, you can make the men speechless and put fear in them only if you will be decent in all manner of life. Though you are the least in creation but you are the great in all things in creation.

It is you that make the world complete in creation. Do not allow weeds grow in your field but build the wall with it and always weed with honesty. Nice but faulty; weak but most influential in all the creation.

In fact, women are like the net which use to snatch the fishes in the sea. They are like trap that can make men powerless but they always fail to trap for good.

Their tricks are for wrong but not right. Means their beauty can influence for good only if they will allow Christ as their leader and guide.

It is my wish that you will love the truth and exchanges your faulty for honesty and weakness for patience that builds good manners.

7. What makes your ladyship sure?

Women need to be careful and considerate. It is not good to eat any food you like, but it is good to eat the food you have been taught to eat. Means do not live as you wish but live according to the principle set up.

What makes you a woman? What ladyship am I talking about? Who is a woman of value? Be a lady involves what? What must a lady be?

You cannot be a lady by misusing your time or regardless the time. Ladyship involves; honesty, forcefulness, industry; update with knowledge and decency. It contains the beauty of character and good manners.

What appears are what is within or the inner being? A good woman appears by the good deeds store up in her heart then reveals good fruits.

The same as a bad woman; you cannot deceive anyone by your act; it will bear the fruit at the end. Faithfulness builds a city and it establishes justice and peace. A good lady appears as a rain that showers the thirsty ground.

She is always alert to help; alert to cheer a heart of trouble, alert to give the best to her colleagues and alert to welcome all people with deep respect. She does not pretend but alert to tell the truth from her heart.

She is friendly and always alerts to welcome. Her appearance speaks about her decency and dignity. She does not entertain evil, yet entertain people with her cheerful words.

It takes kings and queens to reach her concerning of her good name. Means she is not cheap to be cheated and weak to be use by men.

She is meek but not cheap; simple but not as a timid. She is serious and up to work. She avoids laziness and love industry. She cooks well and avoids lazy food on her table. She loves neatness of heart and good outfit.

It takes giants to seek her for presidents and kings. Means it takes well renowned and honorable men to have her to married.

Not that she is unapproachable, approachable but not just anyone. She respect and loves to share her ideas to others. She keeps her beauty name and glory. Means, she fears God and eschew evil.

She avoids lies but always want to tell the truth. She does not allow money to buy her mind but wish to do the right thing for the sake of God.

She cannot be bought or sold. She cannot be enticed by wealth or possessions. She understands and have right mind always. She loves peace and always wants peace for others.

Her friends do not understand her but she knows what to do in each time that maintains her beauty as a being. It does not matter your words proceed out to her; whether good or bad, she can contain it.

All things build her beauty of character and wish to maintain it that way. Means she can cope with all smooth and rough word without hurt. She always loves to learn and search the best for her life and others.

Ladyship involves a lot but it point to two options. What shall be your lot? Where will you stand at the end? It is better lose to your gold than to lose your good name.

Are you a lady? Not just a lady or woman, but what kind of lady are you? Good fruits are stored in good vessels for future use. Will you be profitable at the end? Oh women!

8. Respect and fear God!

What have you done to yourself oh women! What do you want? Look at yourself, is that suits you? Does it fit you? Oh why women? So, you do not respect and does not fear God?

Do you not know there is air all over the globe? Why do you want to pollute the air that belongs to all of us? Be wise and set good example; be light and shine in the darkness for others to see.

Do not identify yourself as a harlot woman. A respectful woman does not dress anyhow; does not paint her mouth and face with pons. Do not take things for granted and never be a suspect for fornication.

Why are you disgracing yourself? It does not suit you. Be ashamed of yourself and bow down your head. What do you want yourself to be? Where from this nasty cloth that you are wearing?

What do you mean? What do you want to show up? Where from this eye lashes and pons? Do you know the beauty than your creator? Do you understand fashion than your maker?

What can you teach Him? What design can you make that supersedes His? Where from this long nails on your fingers? Do you know the best than the Lord God who made heaven and the earth?

What do you mean? Do you not respect and fear the one who made all things? Where from this body shape dresses? What kind of character do you want to play? Where from this long hair arrangements?

What satisfies you? How do you want yourself? Is it fair? Does it glorify God? What do you want to do? What do you know and what have you tested? Is there any sense in what you are doing?

What will be the end? What makeup do you want, which God cannot do for you? There is nothing that satisfies you. Oh my dear women, what do you want to promote? Is it good or evil?

Let me know your stand and then know what I shall say well. What difference do you want to make? What fit your beauty than what God has designed for you?

Say word or two? Answer me well? Let me understands you well. Do you respect? What is this? You are the latest creature; with beauty and glory that makes world complete. It is enough for you but nothing again. You are complete that completes the world made. Your shape; your beauty witnesses your completion.

What do you want to add that surpasses all that God intended for you? Do not go beyond the demarcated line or the boundary that suits your beauty. But accept it; fear and gives thanks to God.

For you do not know what is right and fit than God. What best can you do than your maker? Consider this text and know how to comport yourself. Read 1st Peter 3:1-6

Read;

Wives, likewise, be submissive to your own husbands, that even if some do not obey the word, they, without a word, may be won by the conduct of their wives,

2when they observe your chaste conduct accompanied by fear. 3Do not let your adornment be merely outward—arranging the hair, wearing gold, or putting on fine apparel—

4rather let it be the hidden person of the heart, with the incorruptible beauty of a gentle and quiet spirit, which is very precious in the sight of God.

5For in this manner, in former times, the holy women who trusted in God also adorned themselves, being submissive to their own husbands,

6as Sarah obeyed Abraham, calling him lord, whose daughters you are if you do good and are not afraid with any terror.

Women; you must be respect by your appearance and submissive, those married woman to your husbands. Those who are not married yet must know how to conduct themselves in appearance and behavior.

God will bring every deed into judgment whether good or evil. This world cannot be taken to anywhere and neither can you change the laws that govern the nature.

It has been already done and it cannot be change. You cannot add to yourself a single length nor do yourself good as you think is better than what God have given you. Accept your beauty and thanks God for considering you to be on the planet earth. Respect and fear God and then do the right thing!

9. The Women Proud Acts

The worse of life ever practice and the most disadvantage behavior that cause the doom of life; is thinking of self-beauty or being proud of one's self-in the manner of self-important or agreeable yourself than the other. These acts revolve on ladies (women).

The practice of competition among the women is higher than the men. And the manner, in which it is practice, has caused damage to all people in the world.

Women weakness has damage the world beauty in terms of correct life management. Women always feel proud and wish the acts of flesh than the spiritual.

The girls have picked these acts and want to live by sentiment. There is nothing so dangerous than to feel proud of yourself and behave by your emotion.

Girls sometimes act as if they are on top of everyone. Ladies who enter university level, some regardless their colleagues who haven't. Some women feel proud of their beauty and wants to take advantage in everything concerns life.

Today's young girls have taking illegal track and attitude contrary to life principles and are doing what they like. They have taken their shoulders up and behave like birds fighting on food.

That is, they are always ready to promote evil acts and ready to stand for their right of doing that. Girls always want to challenge themselves and acts as if no one is like them; they feel pompous and want to show off.

You cannot stand well whiles you are on the muddy area. That is, you can't have good atmosphere by your negative attitude and you cannot push without position yourself well.

Means every act in life comes by intent and the result makes the difference. They must be honest and prudent in order to have remarkable name and praise worthy; which is valuable and admire by people.

In fact, life is not fashion. But it is principles and the fate matter. Young ladies must have patient about life and move wisely. They are to take note of every step they make and fixed their steps well.

Girls must be alert about their life and manage it well. All acts have what it takes about life and nothing can be done well without good attention. Your misused life today is the penalty at your future scandal.

Never abuse your life by sexual immorality or other things else and lose your wealth. You can lose your gold because of your acts and dismantle your life diamond hardly to repair or refine as you wish at first.

That is, you cannot have your quality life again if you lose it. You must consider everything you do and beware of the shoes you ware.

That is, be careful about in and out actions and manners. You must build your life with good attitude and special ingredients for your beautiful praise.

Proverb 14:1-4

Says;

The wise woman builds her house, but with her own hands the foolish one tears hers down.

2 Whoever fears the Lord walks uprightly, but those who despise him are devious in their ways.

3 A fool's mouth lashes out with pride, but the lips of the wise protect them.

4 Where there are no oxen, the manger is empty, but from the strength of an ox come abundant harvests.

The effort introduces in everything, erect good or bad fruit but carefulness in doing brings the welcome atmosphere and results in peace life. If you want yourself good, good will come, equally the bad ends the same.

Young women must be careful about in and out actions and make prudent decision for themselves; and never lose the opportunity they have, else they will go through tremors they will never forget.

They must live carefully and watch their acts towards everything they do. Life is not like quiet sleep or resting in the guest house.

Yet it is a continuous fight that needs not rest or stop. One mistake causes much trouble and destroys life ability and brings life penalties.

Currently, ladies have made the world so dirty and have destroyed correct thinking because of their attitude in dress, and they never mind the consequence.

In fact, world today is for the women and the women is for the world! Everything in the world is now moving by the women and the world has damage through the manner of their appearance.

This is true and there is no doubt about it and many of them witness and even make comments on that. It is their news and it bears evidence against them!

If adult women will change their style of living and make good example as prudent women, the young girls will make the world beauty as rosy and the world will take its healthy cloth again. Following the world beauty is nothing but the fear of God makes the difference.

Note this scripture;

Proverbs 31:30, 31

Charm is deceptive, and beauty is fleeting; but a woman who fears the Lord is to be praised.31 Honor her for all that her hands have done, and let her works bring her praise at the city gate.

The acts shown today by many young girls are horrible and it needs attention. The manner in which some of them behave is unacceptable.

When the life takes bad root it goes beyond the margin, and it is difficult to dig for the end. But many of them entertain it. In fact, women are far advance in negative attitudes than men and it is obvious.

They know how to hide sin than digging or searching for gold. Obviously women can control the men by their acts and dismantle the good name ever known.

If the women take off their negative hat, the sun of rain will forever cease and the world we live today will be light of happiness.

What am I want to say; the world we live today can be fair and the best place to stay depends on the style of the women willing to live. The attitude of many young girls has deformed many of the boys today.

In fact, when it comes to the character as we all knew that makes a person. Many women do not care their acts or never mind to show the negative side of it, to disturb their colleagues and are ready even to do more to make it worse. This is true, they mean to sin than to spare.

Further, the women are pretenders or want to show off or pretend to be good-looking. Women are very pretenders and have the deceived acts than men.

Many women acts are deceptions and always want to defend their false acts. The world we live has a lot of lessons and notes to be considered.

This world cannot cover it beauty again till Christ comes and there is no other chance that can be entertain for the best life.

But if care is taking, we will benefit some positive lifestyle. The only thing we can do is to be careful about the way we live and take note about every step we make. The Lord is coming!

Many acts are destroying our being every day and night that result eternal death but the women always entertain it.

In fact, if women will decide to live positive life, this world will somehow turn a bit positive atmosphere and the storms that always take men will semi- cease.

However, life lessons are notes to correct the wrong acts but if we neglect the experience that resulted, then, we cannot cover it again as we wish.

Misuse life have nothing to cover again in the best state as wish but the life well manage can have what it takes. Many girls put their life into second fiddle and wish to act fleshly.

They think that, everything is normal and considered not. Eating as they wish and walk as they like; cloth anyhow and never listen to the advice or take note of the life matters.

Women can change the world; if they consider the life principles and live according to the laws govern the life acts, then nothing will be needed again for best life traffic.

If the women will manage the life according to its best and take care about their acts, then men will be cease from mind murdering and have their being as whole. The Women must consider their acts and live modestly.

Note this scripture:

1Peter 3:1-5

Wives, in the same way submit yourselves to your own husbands so that, if any of them do not believe the word, they may be won over without words by the behavior of their wives,

2 when they see the purity and reverence of your lives. 3 Your beauty should not come from outward adornment, such as elaborate hairstyles and the wearing of gold jewelry or fine clothes.

4 Rather, it should be that of your inner self, the unfading beauty of a gentle and quiet spirit, which is of great worth in God's sight.

5 For this is the way the holy women of the past who put their hope in God used to adorn themselves. They submitted themselves to their own husbands.

There is nothing short in nature, which needs to be modified or refine in other way for the best use. The things created were perfect from the beginning and well please.

But suddenly something strange happened and things created lost the exact state of its nature. Every act has the effect and can be resulted negatively or positively at the end.

One mistake can create damage without remedy and can earn in eternal lose. Women must be carefully considering their actions in any manner of life and they must watch out their dress wearing currently.

The miserable state of the world today stands on the manner of the women clothes themselves. The stylish nature they appear in public causing mind disease and blocking correct nature of thinking.

This increasing the lust of the eye and resulted in shamefulness. There is nothing so dangerous than making yourself stumbling block for others or plan to make people fall by your appearance through pretending.

At the moment, women purposely appear in the manner that cause mental or spiritual fall, to destroy correct thinking and to set trap for people to lose their life.

Women today have totally decided their stand in dressing and have shown the side which they are, and have decides their eternal home by the manner of their cloth.

Never put me wrong, I am telling you the truth. Every dress wear represent the character and the manner of your appearance shows what you have decide.

Many people do not know what they are about in life and what they are doing about life, taking things for granted and behaving as they wish.

Most of the women are so serious to act negatively and never mind to create what will cause harm to other people's life; and many of them are happy in doing that. Your act can decide your destiny and can make negative or positive home for you.

All things done on earth have the peak or low estimate which can complete or incomplete of the project of life been set up.

Women love eyes beauty than inner beauty and promote weeds than the seed. That is, they loved what will destroy few days than what will last long or wish moment than hours or days.

They love food ready to eat, than the food preparing to eat, that is, they want things fast than waiting before the best time and that is their lot that is why we are all suffering today.

Women are the keys and the men are the doors, women can lock and open men in all matters of life and men have no say.

Women have access to life avenues, and they are welcome everywhere in the world because they have the key of access; but they never know because of lack of self-actualization and they lack considering about life issues.

They weigh all things light and considered not the outcome. Women lack spirit of forgiveness and they are also ready to curse than to bless when they are offended.

They lack patience in life but ready to provoke than to make happiness. Many of them are very lazy and not willing to work from heart.

They are gossip and active in making fun of others and to pull down others dignity. All these acts deform their beauty and closed their insight for earning the best life at the end.

Many of them lack understanding and difficult to accept their fault. But women have control, because of their attractive form.

And if care is taking, they can turn the world around in its better state and the world will be partially nice.

As the strong wind sometimes throw out dust to the eyes of the people, so to the women who intentionally dress negatively makes dust around the globe for to hurt many eyes and to destroy the correct thinking with their acts. Women must take care on how they act in all manners of life.

I wonder why women love the world and its goods; that benefit nothing and always hoard up belongings. In fact, this world cannot and will not give anything worthy and help otherwise. But if women will be vigilant and decide what is right about life, then world will shine and favor all of us and the life will be fair. This message needs your consideration!

10. Today's Women conducts

I do not, sometimes, understand women in this world in relation to how they want to appear. In fact, I can say women are the world. I ask myself what women want from this world.

This world is for women. What are the women searching for? What do they want to do? Human appearance makes him a real being. Women do not care for certain appearances in relation to what they wear.

Our world today is moved by women. They do not care about what they wear, whether it is good or bad. Interestingly, they are moving this world into destruction by what they wear.

Some women of today are promoting fornication, because of what they wear. They appear to engage in provocative dances on the dancing floor.

Human beings are, sometimes, known by what they wear. Life in this world is short, and we do not know what is in store for us; that is, no one knows what will happen to him or her.

This world is running out of time. We hear bad news every day. But many women of today do not care about anything concerning life.

The dressing has brought a lot of damage to the human mind, and this has blocked correct thinking, which can bring about wonderful things into our world.

Wearing of indecent clothes lures people, and it has caused a lot of accidents in our world. Women of the day have damaged this world with what they wear. I have a question for them. Who is a Christian? Does Christianity say anything about what women wear?

When you enter the house of God, the same dress which you will see in the world is what you find in the church of God.

Women of today have become promoters of fornication through what they wear. Woman, who is Christian? Woman, what do you want from the world which is passing away?

Today, you cannot differentiate between a Christian woman and a worldly woman. Women have become channels of evil because of their clothing since what you wear defines you.

When you dress badly, you reveal bad character and the bad character reveals bad destiny. There is nothing that identifies a person's character more than the person's adornment. What you wear reveals your character and reflects your status in society.

Sometimes, people are known for their adornment. Many men have become fornicators because of what some women wear.

Women of today have no excuse for what they wear, and they cannot say that worshipping God has nothing to do with how you dress. What you wear is a matter of concern for Christianity.

A Christian who is of good standing can fall because of a woman's indecent dressing. In fact, all dresses identify characters. Accordingly, I can say that an indecent dress is a tool for fornication.

Human beings have lost the covering of glory God endowed us with when the human race sinned and became naked. It was this merciful God who covered our nakedness with proper clothes. If you wear indecent clothes, you promote sin.

Most women promote adultery through their dressing. It is difficult to say something about the clothes women of today wear. This is because these clothes appear almost everywhere.

Many people wear the same clothes to church, parties, clubs, meetings and so on. Today's fashion has brought a lot to confuse other women who want to be modest. Consequently, such women are torn between what is decent and what is socially accepted.

One trait of fashion which some women carelessly follow is wearing a pair of tight trousers that reveal their body contours. This type of clothes promotes fornication and adultery.

The world has become women, and women have become the world. Clothes are characters, and the fashion of the day has become a channel of destruction.

Women must be careful. 'Moreover, the Lord said, because the daughters of Zion are haughty, and walk with stretched-forth necks and wanton eyes... making a tinkling with their feet...' (**Is. 3:16-26**).

All our adornments communicate with our followers and those around us. Wearing of clothes speaks a lot than the waves of the sea; it needs a great amount of carefulness.

The adornment of today's women has destroyed proper communication and has damaged the world's beauty.

The dressing of the day has put our world into a pit of sin, and this is a potential for man's doom. Many of the women of today have caused mind traffic and have damaged a lot of minds for correct thinking.

11. Why marriage was established?

The world was created by God for a purpose; and God is one but with three personal beings. How can you understand this idea or have knowledge of this nature? God dislike loneliness but love relationship and unity.

The absence of beings will result in absence of the world; and no one can live without supporter or associate. It is not good for a man to live alone, and it is also not good for a man to live with trees and animals which cannot talk with him.

The world was created for a man, and the world exists for man sake. All things were created for a purpose and the reason by which it serve. All things are remedy to another, yet all things serve one and another.

If there was no a purpose of creation, yet the creation will not be necessary. We are here for a purpose and live for a reason.

The world is filling with many kinds of things and has the beauty to look at, yet it will be unnecessary when the man wasn't created. Human development and the population of human beings make the world necessary and reasonable.

In order for the world to be necessary, marriage was established; why? Because it is not good for a man to be alone; Trees, Mountains, vegetables, grains, animals and others are man's aids for reasonable life and development.

But these cannot be necessary without human existence. So, in the beginning God created the Heavens and the Earth. The Earth was empty and formless which cannot be explained. But it was arranged for the reason and the benefit of man sake.

The world was filled out with all necessary things in six day by God. The man was created in the image and likeness of God; and he was assigned in the Garden of Eden and was appointed to be overseer of all things which are seen today.

The man named all things and those things are for his joy and development. He was alone and speechless due to lack of partner or helper. Who can move without legs or who can speak or communicate without listener?

It will be purposeless when the man was created alone and then unnecessary to be in the world without a woman or partner. So, it was not good for a man to be alone.

God made a helper fit for him and both became one flesh. Life became necessary for a man when the woman was created. In fact, no one can live happily without associate with all his or her life span.

Yet, Marriage became necessary for man and woman to develop the world through birth. Both became one flesh through marriage. The woman was form from the man and through marriage; the man also can be form from the woman.

As the woman came from the man, so man can also come from the woman through marriage. This is wonderful and deep to understand. Why marriage was established by God? What is the reason? Why marriage must be carefully considered and honored?

The whole human life and development is based on marriage. They were blessed and allow them to multiply and be fruitful; to fill, subdue, replenish, and to have dominion over the earth.

The marriage was established to do away isolation; to bring development and to make the world reasonable to live. Marriage rules must carefully and seriously observe.

It is the basic foundation of human's life and the source of human's families. God is one and the source of all things.

The world and everything in them were created for man and his descendant. For this reason, the man and his wife will leave his father and mother and cleave to his wife and then became one flesh, as God is one.

Marriage is the sign of unity and bond of love which defines the worship and the unity between us and God as our creator. It makes sense to live the world and also produce the fruit of joy and the progress of life.

There is nothing that can be comparing by the reason of unity. It is also a sign that defines the unity between the Father; the Son and the Holy Spirit. The beauty is that, it makes us understand the idea of love and unity that promote progress of life.

So, it is not good for man to be alone. Loneliness kills joy and does away inner and outer beauty. The world became reasonable through marriage establishment.

It is a foundation of human's families and the source of human development. The world was created for a man in the sense of development through marriage institution. In all, the world became active through marriage.

The man (Adam) became speechless due to the absence of woman. Though, he named all things that were created for him. Yet, he became lonely after naming all the things around him.

Can you imagine such a condition of a man at that time? What can you compare? How will you describe? It is not good for man to live alone, I will make him a helper fit for him; said the Lord.

Here, the world was made for the man sake and the woman was made for man as his help mate to prevent loneliness and lack of development. This is great and sensible; else the world would be lifeless and with only one man who cannot develop by his own moves.

Let us not consider marriage as a little thing. The world and its abundance are for man and his wife. God created the man in His likeness and image, man and woman.

They were both naked but not ashamed. The woman was created with the same bone and the flesh of his flesh.

The blood of his blood and with her senses equal to his. The motions are the same and the speech was one with his. She shall be called woman, because she was taken out from the man. Therefore, the man will leave his father and mother and cleaves to his wife and then they become one flesh.

12. How serious marriage is?

The world was built in six days by God and then rested on the seventh day and blessed it. But God designed marriage to be an eternal thing. Yet, sin of a man destroyed everything which God proposed.

Note; marriage was designed to be a world which produce human families proposed by God for eternity. It was an eternal thing which has no end and no one has right to separate it.

The idea was to be as God second home which serve as the unity of love; that confirm the unity between the Father; the Son and the Holy Spirit.

This unity cannot be separated and it is there for eternity. Whatever God made is an eternal thing, but sin caused the change or the damage.

In fact, marriage is not separable; it is bond of love wedded to last eternity. But this idea has been demolished by sin. Now human beings cannot last as designed by God. Yet, the unity remains the same.

It is the foundation that carries the structure; the length and breadth of all human families. So marriage cannot be taken as a mere thing which anyone can carry it.

It is not so at all. The unity that exist God's heads must exist between man and his wife. But what do we see and hear concerning marriages today?

It is sin problem that has brought all these things. What God has joined, let no one separate it. How serious marriage is? How must we take it? What does the marriage stand for? How serious it is?

The world is basically made for man as his eternal home. He was instructed to have dominion over the things in them.

He was designed to live eternally and then develop it for his aid forever. The world was given him as a gift through his life last (eternity).

How can he develop it? Where from the development? God intentionally created the world with raw materials for man. The man was made in the likeness and image of God.

As creator of the Heaven and Earth, He (God) made the image resemble like Him; who can create and care the things that were created in proper way like Him.

So, everything was given to a man to care and manage. Yet, he was single and lonely difficult for him to communicate with those materials around him. The life became tough for him and his joy lost.

Though, he was perfect and able to do everything. Yet, how can he develop and make life dear? In fact, God did something to make the world dear and then to have the leader in everything He made. Not that He forgot to create the man's helper.

God made the age and leadership difference to suit the idea He wanted. So, He (God) made garb or distant between the man and the woman to fulfill the age and leadership differences. That is why He delayed in creating woman for a man.

It is not good for a man to live alone; said the Lord, I will make him helper fit for him. So, woman was made for man as his helper to fulfill his goal as God intended. In order for a man to develop well, the help mate was made for him.

This made the completeness of a man and the world that has been created for him. Therefore, the man will leave his father and mother and to cleave with his wife and they shall become one flesh. So, God intentionally made woman for man as his help mate to develop the world He has made for them.

So, there is no man without woman, and there is no woman without a man. Means the absence of one will be fruitless and empty with no development.

In fact, human family gains hope when the woman was made for man. The world fulfilled her hope through the presence of woman. The joy of the man (Adam) made complete as soon as he saw the woman (Eve).

Oh what a joy! Now the man was contented when he first saw the woman. It is dangerous to take marriage light or a mere thing.

The world became world when the human family was first established by God. It lacks completion when the woman was not yet created.

Therefore, God rested from all His work that He had made on the seventh day and then blessed it. Marriage is the institution of love and unity.

It serves as an example of the unity between God's heads which there is no separation among them as one. This is the purpose that God made the marriage to be.

For this reason, the man and his wife will leave their father and mother and cleave to his wife and then become one flesh. You are my bone and my flesh.

13. You are my bone and flesh

Oh my love! You are my bone and my flesh. You are everything and wealth. You are my second self and joy. Oh dear; you are beautiful! What can I compare with you? What shall I say about you? You are dear and cherish-able.

Adam became shock when he first saw the woman (Eve) approaching him. The woman appearance moves him to talk unexpectedly. He was shock to see such a beautiful appearance resemble to him approaching.

Adam dearly appreciates what God made for him. It makes him move unexpectedly with the words of love and joy. Loneliness kills the souls and damps the spirit. What can you imagine or compare with his joy at that moment?

In fact, woman is the joy of a man. She is the only gift that cannot be share with anyone or exchange for any other thing. She cannot be exchange for anything and she cannot be share with anyone.

She is a wedded being to man with one bone and flesh. She is the latest gift for man that exceeded the entire gift that God had made for man. She is the flesh of a man and bone of his bones. Out of a man the woman was made by God.

She is a man part that made him complete. She is the rib of a man that covers his heart and then protects his life. Without woman, a man cannot be complete.

She is his cloth that covers and the pipe that connect to his heart for the flow of the love of blood to flow well, and then makes his joy complete. She is the dot that completes the man as meaningful sentence.

The bond between man and woman in marriage is greatest than any greatness in human's life. It is a blood and life for eternity.

But sin has broken the profound love and life that it is in the marriage today. Let no one cause alarm that is a mere thing. Never weigh marriage in balance or measured as gold.

It cannot be weighed or measured. It is beyond measure or weight, because it carries nothing but only love; and that is the measure and weight in marriage.

Why? Because love covers everything in human's life. You are my bone and flesh oh dear! The relationship between man and woman is great. The metals that can join well are metals that are with the same fashion and material.

So, the man and woman must hold the same flesh and bone. They hold different nature and different substances. There are many different things in the world that makes the world beautiful.

The trees have their color and nature; rivers have their color and nature, fishes and other animals has their color and nature as well.

There are many different kinds of things in the world. But one thing that we need to note and observe is that, man is the being that resembles God in image and likeness.

Why God made man in His image and likeness? He was made in the likeness and image of God for a reason of to have dominion and rule the world like God. The man holds the glory of God but not with the same flesh and bone.

He was made in resemble in the structure that can move and talk like God but not with the same flesh and bone.

Yet, the woman was made in resemble and with the same flesh; bone and blood. She was made to fit and to support the man with the same image and likeness. This shows the beauty of creation and the love of God for man.

The greatest gift that makes human race so dear is that, they can bring their young ones through sexual intercourse.

Through unity of the man and woman produce fruit of the same kind of their beings. Oh this is dear and awesome! I am your bone and your flesh. Oh my love!

The key that opens unity between man and woman is love. The love is matrix that combines the man and woman into one flesh. Therefore, the man will leave his father and mother and to cleave to his wife and they shall become one flesh.

The man was single when he was created first by his Creator. He was endured with many gifts and good atmosphere.

There are a lot to count with, but one thing makes him lonely. Who will help him to care and develop those things that have been trusted in his hand? This is not his question, yet it is not good a man to live alone.

God made for him a woman, and he said; this at last is bone of my bones and the flesh of my flesh; she shall be called woman, because she was taken out of man. Man and woman is one in marriage, they cannot be distinct.

14. Sex and its purpose

The relation between man and woman is great. In all, it is a peak idea in marriage that man and his wife must have sexual intercourse to produce their young ones. It is an obligation for both mates to act their part when it comes to sex activity.

Sexual intercourse was intentionally made for marriage couples. It is a peak unity act that forms the man and the woman as one. It is a peak mistake to avoid sex in marriage; else it will do away idea of unity as one flesh.

Sexual intercourse maintains the beauty of the couples and then drive bond of love to its highest height. The beauty is that, there is nothing to compare with or describe to this relation, because it makes different of life altogether.

The unity between marriage couples blend by this act and then make it reasonable to live as human beings. Never ever disjoin your marriage through this sex relation.

It is wrong to refuse it when there is no sickness. The production of human beings comes by this action and then paves way for other human beings to see the act of God and the beauty of creation.

It is gate of opportunity for all human beings to be in the world. It is also opens the door of progress of unity of love to stand firm.

As food nourishes and grow the flesh, so sexual intercourse make marriage successful and then grow it as well. It is the rope that binds the love to maintain its seat. As love covers all wrongs, so sex prepares the marriage to stand firm.

Have you ask yourself why God made marriage unique than anything else He created? Why sex is important in marriage? Why sex at all? God created man and woman with two different sex organs.

What is it for? What is the idea behind? Why man and woman, but not man with man or woman with woman? It is contrary to join the same sex organ beings as one when it comes to production of human beings.

It is against God's law and it is an abomination. Two same sexes cannot produce, and it cannot fulfill God's idea for creating the world. Many people have deviated from the idea by which God established marriage.

Others do not honor the sex idea, yet they make it void and useless. The world cannot be the world without people. It is a penalty to misuse sexual intercourse or use it as fun of life when you are not married.

It is purposely made for only married couples but not for unmarried. Human race is originally come from this activity. Sexual intercourse is the pitch of human origin and opportunity to be in the world.

It needs preparation and well balance mind to be in this stage; else it will be abusive and abhorring. Marriage bed must be highly honored to avoid curse and disunity. Let your dance be attractive and interesting to prevent disgrace and misinterpretation.

Means let your partner feels happy and welcome to prevent confusion. Do not put your obligation aside to disturb the other. That is, do your part to support and then make your partner happy in that season.

Manage to keep yourself always for your partner and then fulfill your missions. Means be faithful and maintain your beauty to the end. She is your bones and your flesh. You are her head; shield and eye.

15. The sign of truthfulness

Marriage is a sign of faithfulness to God. It is a sign of truthfulness that maintain our honesty to God. It maintains the beauty of unity and love of God as our duty.

When two live together, means they have agreed and wish to be one in all matters of life. This is the idea that exists between man and his wife and God.

True marriage makes faithfulness and joy. Means it promote unity and progress. God establish marriage to promote faithfulness and unity between two persons. The idea of this institution is to show how man and woman can maintain their faithfulness to God in worship.

Marriage is not just a marriage, but it is a symbol of honesty that individual can show to their colleague and God. It is our duty to stay and maintain our honest to God and neighbor.

As the marriage stands as the sign of honesty, so men must be faithful to God. It is the wish of God that human beings must stay faithful to their fellow and then maintain unity among themselves.

Unity makes progress in life, yet disunity destroys the foundation of truthfulness. It is everyone's duty to stay faithful to maintain unity.

The chaos of the world stands on unfaithfulness. But true unity maintains honesty. Love builds the broken wall and then prepares all things.

If marriage couples will stay faithful to each other, then the world will heal from its sickness.

Every marriage will determine the kind of life or the world we will have when it is establish. Let everyone note that, unfaithfulness in marriage will determine the kind of home they will establish.

Marriage is the key that opens the world destiny. It determines kind of people we will have and the world we shall live. So, if the marriage couples are not faithful, definitely it will produce fake people instead of original ones.

Marriage is life and death matter that determines the end or the kind of home it shall built. The beauty is that, it unites two families together.

Let not anyone enter into marriage with a hurry or unprepared mind. It needs patience and reasonable person to marry, but not the unconcern persons.

Never take marriage as a mere thing; if you do so, you will fail in everything you will intend to do in life.

The world misery today was cause by the unfaithful parent we had at the beginning of the world. Adam and his wife could not sustain their dignity as was required by God.

They failed of their test and then unite with the foreign god. They disobey God and did what they wish. They destroyed what God intend for them and then disgraced themselves.

This caused their sentence of death and the negative life. They lost the big opportunity and the eternal life that God proposed for them.

Today many couples are following the same trend that they passed. The main idea of marriage was lost due to disobedient of our first parents. Now there are a lot of broken marriages cross the world.

This has caused the unfaithfulness to God and our fellow human beings. God established marriage to emphases the truthfulness that exists between Him and us.

It is the sign of honesty and unity between Him and us as His creatures. So, it is possible for couples to live by agreement.

16. The world and its abundant

In the beginning God made Heavens and the Earth, it was dark and deep with waters and formless and empty. It is nothing by it form and indescribable nature. It seems nothing and useless when it was first appeared.

The Spirit of God hover the waters; and then God declared let there be light, and there was light. The Heavens and the Earth was together as one. That is, it was joined and with no separation. I mean, there was no gab between them; shapeless and void.

It contained nothing but waters and deep darkness. What happened and how it was all begun? Why world and its abundance of things which are in different shape and colors? What is the idea? Intentionally, God created the world for human being sake.

It was void and formless with waters and deep darkness. But God took to Himself as Architect and laborer and then prepared it with abundance of goods and ingredients. God divided or separated the Heavens from the Earth and then command the waters to gather into one place for the dry ground to appear. With six days, God did a series of work to fill this world with goods and resources. He causes the Earth to grow with grasses and trees and others things.

As the Earth and Heavens are complete; He made man in His image and likeness. Then on the seventh day, He rested from all the work He had done and blessed the seventh day. Now the world has become home for man to live.

God made a Garden of Eden in east side of this world and placed the man there. It was man first home specially made for him by God within this world. It was gorgeous and full of fruits; seed and shrubs good for food.

There was tree of life and also the tree of knowledge of good and evil. This Garden lacks nothing. I mean all the necessary things were in this home of a man and his wife. The world and everything in them were made for man and his wife for eternity.

There was no sickness or anything that will harm them. All things were for their good, if they will obey all the regulations given to them. There is nothing to harm them, only if they disobey the laws given to them.

Everything is for their good and progress. New home is new life and new life is new home. The joy and progress are food for souls, but the broken spirit rot bones and flesh.

Every new marriage begins new world and creation, and abundant lives are abundant of joy. Difficulties of life make experience but new life makes new home. God made everything for man and his wife. So, marriage needs new world and abundance of goods and resources.

As marriage institution demands, so every new marriage couples needs their share. The world and everything that is in them are for man and his wife. Yet every new family needs to have their needs that marriage demands.

It is their rights and needs that built their family or home. So, this world is purposely created for marriage couples. That is, the man and his wife. Everything in the world is for man and his wife.

The trees; the waters, the animals, the hills and everything that eye can see. Some are for food; some are for dresses, some are for shelters and so on.

God blessed marriage, and the couples duty is to multiply, subdue and replenish. If marriage couples will live faithfully and then stay as the marriage rules demand, blesses shall overshadow them and then unity and love will last eternally.

They shall have their food in due time and nothing shall offend them. Their children shall prosper and their children's children will be the stars among thousands. Who does not love happy home? Who wants to be poor in all his or her life?

God knows the kind of thoughts He has for us; it is the thoughts of peace but not of evil, to give us hope and greatest future. He created the world for every man and his wife. He knows them and then wishes them good and great future.

Marriage is not a mere thing that we should joke with. It is sign of love; duty and unity between us and God as His creatures.

The world and its abundance are for man and his wife. Oh darling! Let's give thanks to the Lord God who created Heavens and the Earth, for He is mercy and good!

17. Life and death matter

Marriage cannot be separated when it is wedded. It is the door that no one can open when it is closed. It is not returnable life when you entered. It demand eternity of life and bond which cannot be deny.

It has the peak of thoughtful ground and the point of no return. It demands single of mind and faithful to duty. Let no one enter without thought or haste. It is a life and death matter that needs thoughts and vigilance.

I mean unplanned marriages can decide dreadful destiny for others. One thing everyone who is about to marry must know or put in mind or ask is that, where will this relationship will end me? How prepared I am?

Is that woman or man fit for me? Will he or she understand? Can I be able to cope with all circumstances that come away? Who should I marry? How helpful will be this marriage?

In fact, all these questions are needful, and you must ask yourself before entering. Marriage is love relating to man and woman. It is a journey with no return and decision you cannot reject.

It is not a joke and cannot be joke with. It is serious matter and life decision. Let no one take as anything without consequence. It has the result of life or death matters.

Many people go into marriage without thinking. Others marry because of lust and mercy. Some people also take marriage as a mere thing. It is better to be single than to marry to the one that lacks understanding.

In fact, marriage is not there for anyone, but it is there for those who are prepared and has given. It is a gift, and it is for those who have been given. It is not anyone who can marry but those who it has been given. It is the service of God that defines faithfulness in all things.

Marriage is not just a gift without management or law. It has a duty and the laws that govern it. It is not just free gift which has no accountability. It is a gift with accountability and it needs to progress and then bears fruit.

What I have seen is that, many people take marriage as a mere thing that has no value. Others think that, you can marry as many as you want. It is not so and big no!

Marriage stands for worship and the sign between us and God. Anyone who missuses marriage as nothing or breaks it, honored gods, instead of God. He, who makes marriage void, breaks the unity between God and man; and then also takes God as nothing!

Let not anyone take marriage as nothing or dishonored marriage bed. It is a sin against God's law and then disgraces Him. *The world and its abundance were made for marriage couples or man and his wife. It is penalty to take marriage as little thing. If you do that, you dishonored God and make His work useless.*

My brother or sister, do not joke with marriage rules or take as a mere thing. It is not, it is life, and it is about human families and the peak idea by which the world was made by God! It is a life; family and the world which God made.

The unity between God and man, fulfill by marriage institution. When anyone enters, he should not break or return. If you break or do so, you dismantle the other part of your flesh or make it void or useless.

Note; let's assuming that you are alone, and you do not have anyone with you. Will you be able to survive without helper?

Or will you avoid the gift made for your progress or will you prevent the gift that will answer your lowliness from your Creator? Marriage institution is not anything else; yet it is an idea by which the world was made.

So, Adam and his wife was the peak object of creation. The world was made for them and they are the beneficial of those things that were made. Their duty is to care and manage those things that were made and then to multiply; subdue and replenish.

Let no one break what God has joined. Our duty is to make it useful or profitable. The man and the woman were the crown beings that make the things that were made useful.

Married couples are legally akin to themselves and there is no way for them to separate. Else, they should remain single; if they dare.

Marriage is bond and it cannot be separated. Let everyone must notice this, before they get themselves involve. Else those people must remain single. That is, better and acceptable by God than marry and then break it.

18. Oh my dear!

Love covers everything and love is greatest of all things. What shall it break this bond oh my dear? You are my part and my second self. You are my bones and my flesh, oh my darling! You are mine and I am yours.

You are my heart and eyes. You are my half that makes me complete. Oh dear how can I live without you? You are the stream that supports my life. You build me with your cheerful words. I cannot live without you oh my love.

You are wonderfully made and beautiful. What can exchange the love I have for you? Oh my wealth! My love for you is great! It is deep than the deepest. Your love is great and awesome. You are the song of my mouth and the food that nourish my flesh.

The burden of soul lifts by true love and covers all wrongs. You are my dear and thoughts each day. Who will I call, if there is no helper? Who can live without helper?

Your absence makes me lowly and incomplete. What can I do without you oh my love? You are my backbone that supports my whole being. You are my rib that covers my heart. Oh dear! When will you come?

I need your presence and love; my shelter and comfort. You are dear to me and wealth for my lives. You are the pool of water that refreshes my flesh and the water quenches my thirst.

Oh my love, you are beautiful! Many people do not understand marriage. Others take it as a light thing. It is difficult to have a right and understandable partner.

Wrong partners have made some marriages wreck and disturbing. Unplanned marriage has breaks many people heart. But God gives understanding woman to those who call and wait for Him.

We all need to be careful and wait. Do not rush into marriage and never marry through lust of flesh. Everyone must note this; it is a grave mistake to seek woman without allowing God to find a right partner fit for you.

Adam did not request a woman from God, but it is God who made woman for Adam. Now it has become the norm for every man to marry a woman, as it is planned by God.

It is not good for a man to live alone. Though, it is now part of us to marry, but it is mistake to choose woman without God concern. Else you will choose a wrong partner to wreck your life, if it is not God's mercy.

Let everyone note that, it is God who gives right partner that fit for man or woman. It is good to seeking God concerning the woman He want for you; because it is God who gives understanding woman.

Let no one rush into marriage without consulting God about it. Today many people are suffering through marriage they been to.

Others have repented from the marriage they engage themselves. Some also are crying because of wrong partners they married. Some are mismatch and others are horrible to look at.

Do not kill yourself through wrong partner, ask God and then wait for Him. They that wait upon the Lord shall renew their strength and shall mount like eagle.

They shall be like river of life that flows and quench and comfort those who are thirsty. You need to pray and wait for God concerning your right partner fit for you. Do not enter into marriage without thinking, yet open your eyes and then make your eternal destiny decision.

For Good Living; salvation and Knowledge Gain!
B. B. S. LIFE BOOKS.

Also by Bernard Benson Sarfo

The Fact Among Facts (1st)
The Fact Among Facts

Standalone
The Youth Murderer
Be Original Not a Copy
The Christians Science or Scholarship
Precious than Paradise
Habit Makes Future
A shelter from storm and rain
The Science of Life
The Strongest Lion Knockback
The Perfect and Inspiring City
Above Hope, Faith and Love
The Hero's Brave Decisions
The Weakest Among Plants
The Hero's Brave Decisions
Doing Above The Ability
The Wisdom Beyond Power And Greatness
Heavier Than the Heavens
The Academics Brains and Recreation Logics
The Strange Voice

The Chaotic World
Don't Miss Your Flight
Let the Nations Ponder
You Are Your Thoughts
I AM has sent me to you
Life Tools
The Fact Among Facts
You Are Glorified
The Life Cinema
The Victims of Lifelong Slavery
The Beauty behind Her Ladyship

About the Author

Bernard Benson Sarfo is an acquainted architectural designer and a motivational speaker.He is a gifted teacher who continues to motivate and encourage many.

Read more at https://www.amazon.com//author/bbslifebooks.